Goofy
Guinea
Pigs

Mary Elizabeth Salzmann
AUTHOR

C.A. Nobens
ILLUSTRATOR

Consulting Editor, Diane Craig, M.A./Reading Specialist

ABDO
Publishing Company

Published by ABDO Publishing Company, 4940 Viking Drive, Edina, Minnesota 55435.

Printed in the United States.

CREDITS

Edited by: Pam Price

Concept Development: Nancy Tuminelly

Cover and Interior Design and Production: Mighty Media

Photo Credits: Corbis Images, Labat & Rouquette/PHONE/BIOS/Peter Arnold, Inc., ShutterStock

LIBRARY OF CONGRESS CATALOGING-IN-PUBLICATION DATA

Salzmann, Mary Elizabeth, 1968-
 Goofy guinea pigs / Mary Elizabeth Salzmann ; illustrated by C.A. Nobens.
   p. cm. -- (Perfect pets)
 ISBN-13: 978-1-59928-749-2
 ISBN-10: 1-59928-749-8
 1. Guinea pigs as pets--Juvenile literature. I. Nobens, C.A., ill. II. Title.
 SF459.G9S25 2007
 636.935'92--dc22
                          2006034401

SandCastle™ books are created by a professional team of educators, reading specialists, and content developers around five essential components—phonemic awareness, phonics, vocabulary, text comprehension, and fluency—to assist young readers as they develop reading skills and strategies and increase their general knowledge. All books are written, reviewed, and leveled for guided reading, early reading intervention, and Accelerated Reader® programs for use in shared, guided, and independent reading and writing activities to support a balanced approach to literacy instruction.

SandCastle Level: Transitional

LET US KNOW

SandCastle would like to hear your stories about reading this book. What is your favorite page? Was there something hard that you needed help with? Share the ups and downs of learning to read. We want to hear from you! To get posted on the ABDO Publishing Company Web site, send us e-mail at:

sandcastle@abdopublishing.com

GUINEA PIGS

Guinea pigs are active animals. They run, play, jump, and make funny squeals and squeaks. They can be cute, fun, goofy pets.

Natalie feeds her guinea pig special food that has alfalfa in it. She makes sure the water bottle is full too.

Fresh fruit is also good for guinea pigs. Xavier gives his guinea pig a slice of apple.

Autumn cleans her guinea pig's cage every week. She covers the floor of the cage with hay.

Aiden plays with his guinea pig in the yard so she can graze and get some exercise. He has an enclosure for her so she won't get lost or hurt.

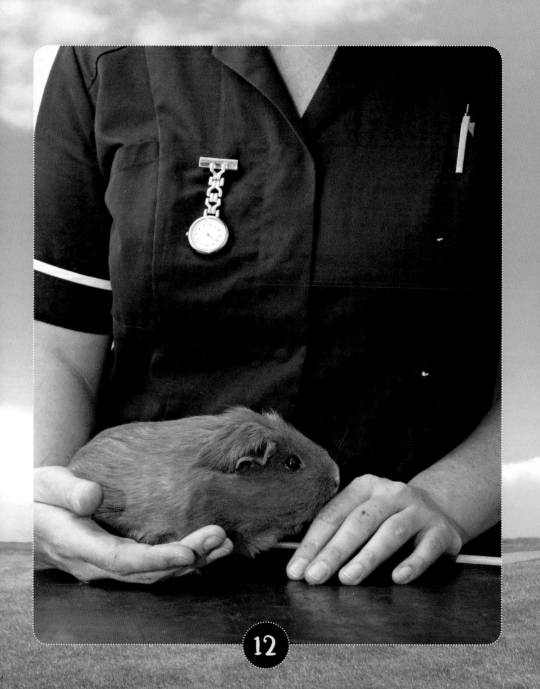

Jesse takes his guinea pig to a veterinarian. The vet checks the guinea pig's teeth.

A Guinea Pig Story

Mary gets her
guinea pig a new toy,
one she thinks Ginger
will really enjoy.

The toy is a large
exercise ball.
She puts Ginger inside
and lets her go in the hall.

14

Ginger quickly
figures it out.
She moves her feet
and rolls about.

All the way down
the hall she goes,
rolling right over
Mary's toes.

When she reaches the
end, she takes a right.
Then Ginger rolls
right out of sight.

"Oh no!" Mary says,
looking high and low.
"Where did that
goofy guinea pig go?"

19

When Mary gets on her
hands and knees,
she sees Ginger under the
bed with the dust bunnies.

She says, "I'm glad you
like the ball, it's true.
But clearly I'll have to
keep a closer eye on you!"

Fun facts

Cavy is another name for guinea pig.

Guinea pigs are not related to pigs. They are rodents, like mice, rats, and hamsters.

Guinea pigs have fur and teeth when they are born.

Guinea pigs' teeth never stop growing. If they don't gnaw on hard objects, their teeth can grow so long that they can't eat.

Guinea pigs originated in South America. Dutch and English traders brought them to Europe, where they became popular pets.

Glossary

active – moving around quickly and often.

bottle – A glass or plastic container with a narrow neck and mouth and no handle.

dust bunny – a clump of dust, lint, and hair that forms under furniture.

enclosure – a device such as a fence or a wall used to confine something.

graze – to eat growing grasses and plants.

slice – a thin piece cut from something.

squeal – a loud, high-pitched cry or sound.

veterinarian – a doctor who takes care of animals.

About SandCastle™

A professional team of educators, reading specialists, and content developers created the SandCastle™ series to support young readers as they develop reading skills and strategies and increase their general knowledge. The SandCastle™ series has four levels that correspond to early literacy development in young children. The levels are provided to help teachers and parents select appropriate books for young readers.

Emerging Readers
(no flags)

Beginning Readers
(1 flag)

Transitional Readers
(2 flags)

Fluent Readers
(3 flags)

These levels are meant only as a guide. All levels are subject to change.

To see a complete list of SandCastle™ books and other nonfiction titles from ABDO Publishing Company, visit **www.abdopublishing.com** or contact us at: 4940 Viking Drive, Edina, Minnesota 55435 • 1-800-800-1312 • fax: 1-952-831-1632